W9-AET-971

DAY BY DAY WITH...

MISSY FRANKLIN

BY
TAMMY GAGNE

Mitchell Lane
PUBLISHERS
P.O. Box 196
Hockessin, Delaware 19707
Visit us on the web: www.mitchelllane.com
Comments? Email us:
mitchelllane@mitchelllane.com

Mitchell Lane
PUBLISHERS

Printing   1   2   3   4   5   6   7   8   9

RANDY'S CORNER

DAY BY DAY WITH. . .

Alex Morgan	Manny Machado
Beyoncé	Mia Hamm
Bindi Sue Irwin	Miley Cyrus
Chloë Moretz	Missy Franklin
Dwayne "The Rock" Johnson	Selena Gomez
Eli Manning	Shaun White
Gabby Douglas	Stephen Hillenburg
Justin Bieber	Taylor Swift
LeBron James	Willow Smith

Library of Congress Cataloging-in-Publication Data
Gagne, Tammy.
  Day by day with Missy Franklin / by Tammy Gagne.
    pages cm. — (Randy's corner)
  Includes bibliographical references and index.
  ISBN 978-1-61228-453-8 (library bound)
  1. Franklin, Missy, 1995– —Juvenile literature. 2. Women swimmers—United States—Biography—Juvenile literature. 3. Women Olympic athletes—United States—Biography—Juvenile literature. I. Title.
  GV838.F69G34 2014
  797.2'1092—dc23
  [B]
                                                                    2013023048
eBook ISBN: 9781612285122

ABOUT THE AUTHOR: Tammy Gagne has written dozens of books for children, including *Day by Day with Justin Bieber* and *What It's Like to Be Oscar De La Hoya*. One of her favorite pastimes is visiting schools to speak to kids about the writing process.

PUBLISHER'S NOTE: The following story has been thoroughly researched and to the best of our knowledge represents a true story. While every possible effort has been made to ensure accuracy, the publisher will not assume liability for damages caused by inaccuracies in the data and makes no warranty on the accuracy of the information contained herein. This story has not been authorized or endorsed by Missy Franklin.

DAY BY DAY WITH
MISSY
FRANKLIN

BRONZE
MEDALIST
AYA
TERAKAWA

In 2012, Missy Franklin competed in the Olympic Games. She was the first American woman ever to swim in seven events at the Olympics! She could have competed for Canada. Both her parents are from that country. But Missy was born in Pasadena, California, on May 10, 1995. She wanted to represent the United States.

Missy's full name is Melissa Jeanette Franklin. But many people call her "Missy the Missile." That's because she moves very quickly through the water when she swims.

The 17-year-old set a world record in the women's 200-meter backstroke at the London Olympics. She finished the race in 2:04.06 (two minutes and just over four seconds).

MISSY FRANKLIN SMILES
AFTER WINNING THE
WOMEN'S 100-METER
BACKSTROKE

Missy also helped her team set a world record in her final relay race at the games. Team USA earned gold in the race when they finished in 3:52.05 (three minutes and just over 52 seconds). These weren't the only two medals Missy would bring home from London, though.

MISSY AND HER USA TEAMMATES REBECCA SONI, DANA VOLLMER, AND ALLISON SCHMITT POSE WITH THEIR MEDALS. THE TEAM WON GOLD IN THE WOMEN'S 4X100-METER MEDLEY RELAY FINAL DURING THE 2012 OLYMPICS IN LONDON, ENGLAND.

D.A. FRANKLIN (MOTHER)

Missy's parents, Dick and D.A. Franklin, learned that their daughter was a gifted swimmer when she was just two years old. Missy was in the water with her mother when a beautiful fish caught Missy's eye.

MISSY WAS BORN IN PASADENA, CALIFORNIA. SHE AND HER FAMILY LATER MOVED TO DENVER, COLORADO.

She immediately chased after it. When D.A. couldn't catch her daughter, she screamed. Dick had to swim about 35 feet into the ocean to catch up with the toddler.

When the family took vacations, the only thing young Missy wanted to do was swim. Her dad told *The Washington Post,* "It went on, not for an hour or two hours, it just went on all day, all week. It was the water and nothing else."

By the time she was five, Missy was swimming with the Rocky Mountain Swim League in Colorado.

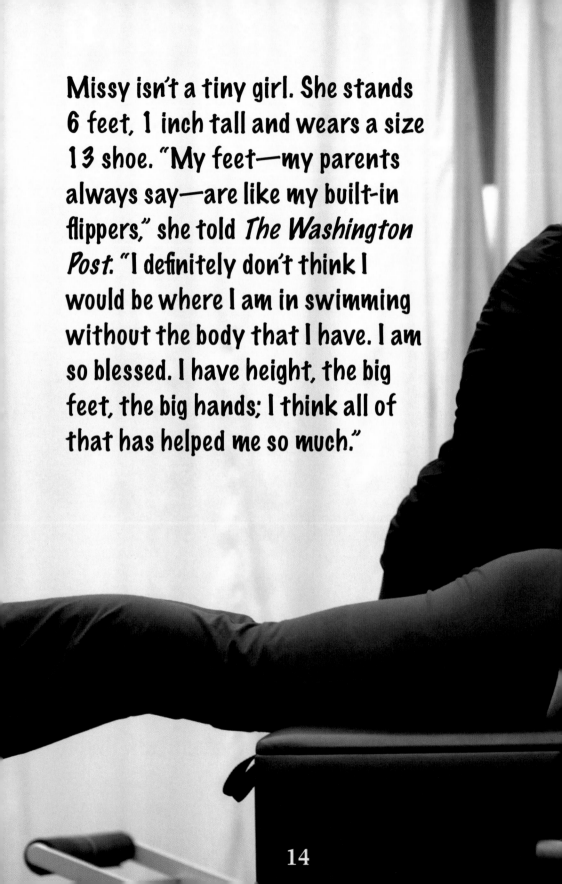

Missy isn't a tiny girl. She stands 6 feet, 1 inch tall and wears a size 13 shoe. "My feet—my parents always say—are like my built-in flippers," she told *The Washington Post.* "I definitely don't think I would be where I am in swimming without the body that I have. I am so blessed. I have height, the big feet, the big hands; I think all of that has helped me so much."

Glamour magazine named Missy one of its Women of the Year in December 2012. Olympic gymnast Gabrielle Douglas, runner Allyson Felix, Judo player Kayla Harrison, and soccer player Carli Lloyd were also included. The American women brought home more medals from London than the men did. Missy alone earned four golds and a bronze in the games.

17

When the London Olympics ended, Missy was filled with emotions. "I'm going to miss this so much," she told *The Denver Post.* "I'm so excited that I'll get to spend a little time with my family and explore London a little bit, but I'm sad. I'm so sad it's all over. I've learned so much from this experience."

Since Missy returned home from London, she has gotten to do some pretty amazing things.

On September 22, 2012, she threw out the first pitch in a game between the Arizona Diamondbacks and the Colorado Rockies.

After the Olympics, Missy appeared on *The Tonight Show with Jay Leno*. She said her favorite part was getting to see his famous car collection.

MISSY'S FOUR GOLD MEDALS AND ONE BRONZE MEDAL

XXX Olympiad London 2012

"I'm a huge fan of *Chitty Chitty Bang Bang*," Missy told *The Denver Post*. "That's one of my favorite movies of all time. And he has so many cars that look exactly like Chitty."

In 2011 Missy and fellow swimmers Natalie Coughlin, Dana Vollmer, and Rebecca Soni won the Golden Goggle Award for Relay Performance of the Year.

Missy was named Female Athlete of the Year at the annual Golden Goggle Awards in 2012. The Golden Goggles are the highest awards in American swimming. She was excited to receive the award. But she told the audience that she was even more thankful for her family, her teammates, and her coach!

Many companies pay professional athletes a lot of money to advertise their products. Missy could earn millions of dollars by appearing in commercials or on cereal boxes. But once athletes turn professional, they can no longer compete at the amateur level. Competing in college is important to Missy, so she has turned that money down.

MISSY SHOWS HER OLYMPIC GOLD MEDAL TO MAKENNA WALLIN AT THE CHILDREN'S HOSPITAL IN AURORA, COLORADO. MISSY AND OTHER MEMBERS OF THE STARS SWIM TEAM STOPPED BY THE HOSPITAL DURING THE HOLIDAYS TO RAISE THE SPIRITS OF MAKENNA AND THE OTHER PATIENTS, THEIR FAMILIES, AND HOSPITAL STAFF MEMBERS.

MISSY'S MOM

Missy may not be ready to sell her image to make big bucks for herself. But she is more than willing to donate her time for a good cause. On September 7, 2012, she appeared on Stand Up To Cancer, a television show that raised money for cancer research.

Missy doesn't spend all of her time swimming or appearing on television. She announced that she would be starting college in 2013 at the University of California at Berkeley. The school's swim team is coached by Teri McKeever. She was also the coach for the US Olympic women's team.

MISSY AT HER DESK IN HISTORY CLASS

MISSY SWAM ON THE REGIS HIGH SCHOOL SWIM TEAM

MISSY SIGNS AN AUTOGRAPH FOR A FAN

The 2016 Summer Olympics will be held in Rio de Janeiro, Brazil. Missy is excited for the chance to compete there. Her parents may also make the trip to cheer her on. Whether she comes home with more medals or not, Missy knows she is already very lucky. As she told *The Denver Post,* "No matter how I swim, . . . I'm still going to have the best family in the world."

31

FURTHER READING

BOOKS

Brassey, Richard. *The Story of the Olympics*. London, UK: Orion Children's Books, 2011.

Miller, Amanda. *Let's Talk Swimming*. New York: Children's Press, 2009.

Newsham, Gavin. *The London 2012 Games Superstars*. London, UK: Carlton Books, 2013.

ON THE INTERNET

Olympic.org: "Missy Franklin" http://www.olympic.org/missy-franklin

Team USA: "Missy Franklin Going for the Gold." http://www.teamusa.org/~/link. aspx?_id=16A87FAF2D9542808CB1F104F28 7BC2E&_z=z

USA Swimming: "Missy Franklin" http://www.usaswimming.org/ missyfranklin

WORKS CONSULTED

Auerbach, Nicole. "USA's Missy Franklin Wins Another Gold, Sets World Record." *USA Today*, August 4, 2012.

Biography.com. "Missy Franklin." http://www.biography.com/people/ missy-franklin-20903291

Cohen, Rachel. "Phelps, Franklin Big Winners at Golden Goggles." The Associated Press, November 19, 2012.

Dolak, Kevin. "Missy Franklin: New Queen of Swimming Takes First Individual Gold Medal." ABC News, July 31, 2012.

Harish, Alon. "Missy Franklin Wants to Swim in College, Put Off Endorsement Fortunes." ABC News, August 4, 2012.

Henderson, John. "Family Matters at Heart: Missy Franklin Has Ascended to Great Heights as a Swimmer, But It's Her Parents Who Keep Her Grounded." *The Denver Post*, May 13, 2012.

Henderson, John. "Franklin a Golden Glow from Sea to Shining Sea: Drop Head Goes in Here Please and Thank You Very Much." *The Denver Post*, September 6, 2012.

Henderson, John. "Missy USA: Centennial Swimmer Ends Games as New Face of U.S. Swimming." *The Denver Post*, August 5, 2012.

Shipley, Amy. "Missy Franklin Has Body Built for Speed." *The Washington Post*, March 21, 2012.

Swimming World Magazine. "Missy Franklin Named One of Glamour Magazine's Women of the Year." November 1, 2012. http://www.swimmingworldmagazine. com/lane9/news/USA/32487.asp

Warren, Lydia. "It's Missy Mania!" Mail Online, July 31, 2012. http://www. dailymail.co.uk/news/article-2181589/ Missy-Franklin-From-childhood-Olympic-gold.html

INDEX